what you don't need
to make the projects in this book:

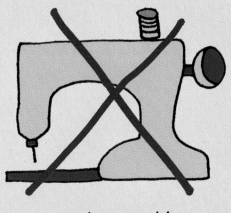

a sewing machine

CHAPTER ONE

the supplies

A Cute Basket Is Key

When you think "sewing kit," do you think of Grandma's ratty old basket? Or one of those mini plastic boxes with seven little teeny-tiny pieces of cardboard covered in about a foot's worth of thread? If so, it's time you rethink the sewing kit. When complete, it can and should be one of your most prized possessions. Sewing kits can get you out of tight binds and minor jams, they can revamp your entire wardrobe, they can fix whatever's broken. In other words, they rock. So let's get yours rolling.

Sewing kits need, first and foremost, a vessel. A place to store your stash. Grandma used a basket, and there's nothing wrong with that. But forgo the doilies and old French lace, please—they're just too stuffy.

A lunch box—can be the old metal variety or a cute kiddie plastic one

A shoe box—plastered with magazine clippings, of course

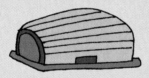

A bread box, preferably one with a lid

A fishing tackle box—particularly apropos thanks to all the little compartments originally designed for nasty hooks and smelly bait

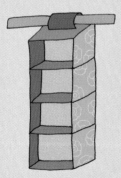

One of those **hanging shoe organizers with pockets;** just stuff your sewing stuff where sneaks would have been

A used, yet clean, **soup pot, stockpot, or Crock-Pot** with a cover (I'm not kidding)

Any container that can comfortably hold about a lunch box worth of goodies.

Feel free to decorate said container with glued-on photos and ribbons, paint, and nail polish. Put your name on the box or basket or soup pot, and own it with pride!

What Makes Up A Sewing Kit?

You could spend days filling your vessel with gadgets and doohickeys. You could easily fill a large Igloo cooler to the rim with sewing paraphernalia, but who needs that, and where would you put it? No, a few key things are all you need. Most of this stuff can be found at any mega-drugstore. If not, get thee to a fabric store pronto.

1. **Scissors:** Sure, a nice, expensive, extra-sharp pair is handy but also dangerous (especially if you have little sisters and brothers). A standard pair of scissors will do nicely. But use them only for sewing and not on paper or hair—that will help keep them sharp.

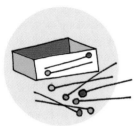

2. **A box of pins:** This is bang for your buck. You can get like a zillion of these babies for around seventy-nine cents. Okay, maybe not a zillion, but close.

. . . .

3. **A seam ripper:** One of the aforementioned "doohickeys," but this one is valuable. It's pointy with a little hook, and it rips open seams, just like the name says. We'll be ripping open a lot of seams in this book. However, if you don't have a seam ripper, you could, in a pinch, substitute a small pair of scissors.

. . . .

4. **An assortment of thread:** A few basic colors are all you really need. You might have to go to a fabric store or craft store to get decent thread (it stinks when your thread keeps breaking every time you pull tight). Thread comes in a ton of varieties, from cotton to poly to bonded nylon; there is embroidery thread, Kevlar thread, Nomex thread— oh, who cares. For these projects stick to classic cotton or poly.

. . . .

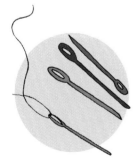

5. **Needles:** They come in packages of assorted sizes that are just perfect for our assorted needs!

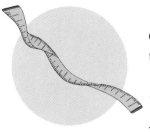

6. **A Tape Measure:** Thin and papery and long, it's really just a flexible ruler.

. . . .

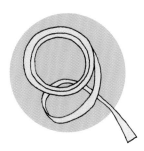

7. **Steam-A-Seam** or some other **paper-backed, iron-on fusible web tape:** Since we're creating all these projects without the benefit of a sewing machine, this stuff is gold. It's like really good double-sided tape that becomes so sticky when heated with an iron that you can hem with it, glue with it, create patches with it—do just about anything with it. And since we'll be using quite a lot of it, it's helpful for you to know how to shop for it. Steam-A-Seam, an actual name brand that's great, most often comes in long, skinny pieces. But you can buy any generic fusible web tape, also called "fusible web appliqué," which comes in a wide roll. You can sometimes even buy it by the yard—and it'll cost you less than five bucks. The best thing about this magical, paper-backed, iron-on product? It requires no needle and thread!

Those are the necessities. You don't need anything else in your kit. But here are **a few extras** that might make life easier and more fun.

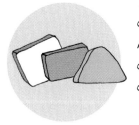

1. **A pincushion** for all those pins: You could even sew one up yourself. (Read ahead and you'll see how in Chapter 3!)

2. **A thimble:** Thimbles are those funny little metal hats for your thumbs. When you're sewing through thick fabric like denim or making felt or velvet flowers, one of these doohickeys will shield your delicate thumbs from the sharp needle.

3. **Tailor's chalk:** Occasionally, you'll need to draw a line on your fabric to mark where you should cut. A pencil creates an oh-so-faint line, often too light a line for the naked eye to see. Tailor's chalk makes a nice, obvious line that can be easily wiped away.

ode to an Iron

The warmth that projects from your metal core

Makes my projects crisp and pressed,

Makes my seams flat and square,

Makes my crafty heart zing!

Careful I am, always

Never forgetting to turn you off,

Always putting you in your safe place,

Where I shall find you again, tomorrow.

4. **Pinking shears:** Essentially scissors with zigzag edges, they cut a cute, country-bumpkin-meets-punk-rock edge. Oh, the fun you can have with pinking shears!

. . . .

5. Beautiful ribbons, glamorous sequins, hipster patches, vintage buttons...but more on those later, in Chapter 11.

CHAPTER TWO

sewing basics

The Hand Jive

Sewing machines are overrated. With your hands and the aforementioned handy-dandy sewing kit, you can create fashionista masterpieces. (Say that five times fast.) You've just got to know how to push that needle.

Threading the Needle: Be sure to place yourself in a well-lit room. Grab a needle (a medium-size one is a great start) and a long piece of thread. Thread can be wily, and that hole is soooo small! So cut the end of your piece of thread at an angle, and you'll have a sharper point to work with. A little spit—I mean, a teeny-tiny amount—on the end of the thread doesn't hurt. It'll help smooth the end of your thread into a really neat point. When you're ready, thread away.

Once you've got the tip of your thread through the hole, you have two choices:

A) Pull the thread all the way through the hole in the needle (that would be called "the eye") so its ends meet, then tie the ends into a knot. Make several more knots. The goal is for the knot to be larger than the hole. This approach is good when you need superstrong stitches, as the thread will be doubled in width.

or

B) Pull the thread through just enough so that the short end is about 6 inches long. Then knot the long end. Tie it several times so that your knot is larger than your needle's eye. You are now ready to sew!

- -

There are four basic stitches that the hand seamstress must know.

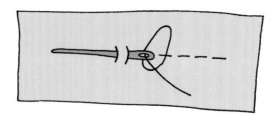

1. **The Straight Stitch:** This is the basic stitch used most often, and as the name implies, it's fairly straightforward. The smaller you make the stitch, the stronger your seam will be.

Start by poking the threaded needle through the fabric from the underside till the knot stops it dead in its tracks. Bring the needle down into the fabric just a quarter of an inch (or even less) away from where you first poked through. Pull firmly but not tightly—you know the diff, right? Keep doing this in even increments along your seam line. Try to keep it very straight. Voila, you're sewing!

Sometimes when I know my stitches are going to show, I like to vary the stitch length. I make one long stitch, then a tiny stitch, then a long stitch, then a tiny stitch to create a pattern as I go.

. . . .

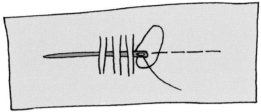

2. **The Running Stitch:** This is the straight stitch's fancy little sister. We use this for making gathers and lovely little pleats. It also goes by the name "basting."

Like the straight stitch, you start by poking the threaded needle through the fabric from the underside, but you do not—I repeat, do not—pull the needle all the way through. Instead, you make several little stitches and hold them right there on the needle. The point of the needle will go in the fabric and then come up the other side, keeping the stitches actually on the needle. When the needle is full (anywhere from three to five full stitches should do the trick), pull your needle out till the knot stops you quick. Pull your thread with a firm but gentle hand.

Presto, instant gathers!

Since this stitch goes lickety-split fast, many people use this as a way to test whether or not they'll like their garments. You could baste your seams to make sure the project is all well and good before you go to the trouble of sewing neat seams. By basting, you can try your soon-to-be-new shirt on, and then go back and do a stronger straight or backstitch over the seam to finish it up.

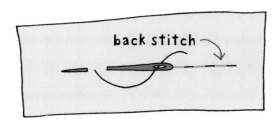

back stitch

3. **The Backstitch:** Someone could have come up with better names for these stitches, don't you think?

This stitch is perfect when you need a supersturdy seam. Make a single, classic straight stitch. Let's say, for example, it's a quarter inch long. Poke the needle back up through the fabric—in this case, a quarter inch past where your straight stitch ended. Now bring the needle down where your first stitch ended, essentially moving backward and closing the gap between the stitches. Repeat. It's a forward, backward, forward, backward motion, and it makes for a nice, tight bond.

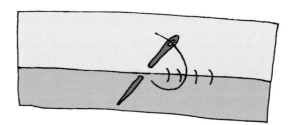

4. **The Hemstitch:** Surprise! This stitch is for hemming, as in the bottom of the your pants, skirts, dresses, and tops.

Start by making a small fold in the fabric, hiding the raggedy raw edge. Press it with an iron. Then make another fold, once again ironing it down. Stick the point of the needle inside the hem and pull it through. We do this to hide the knot. Imagine the edge of the hem as a line. You want to make teeny-tiny diagonal stitches along that line. But you don't want to go through the fabric carelessly. Instead, you poke the needle through the fabric gingerly. The goal is to really get only a couple of threads of the fabric with each stitch. Push the needle back down into the hem fold, but not all the way. Pull it out from under the fold. Keep going, repeating these steps. If you keep the stitches small, you'll end up with a nearly invisible stitch on the front side.

Pretty nifty, huh?

CHAPTER THREE
the pincushion

Now You're Ready for Projects Galore.
Toughen Up Those Thumbs, We're Gonna Sew!

The Perfect First Sewing Project: A Pincushion!

Sure, you could buy one of those cute but plain apple pincushions—or you can craft your very own one-of-a-kind pincushion. You can practice your newfound stitchery, and if the thing isn't perfect, no problem—it's a pincushion! Plus, if you give up sewing next week, just remove the pins, name her "Molly," and pass her on to your little sister or cousin as their newest and dearest toy.

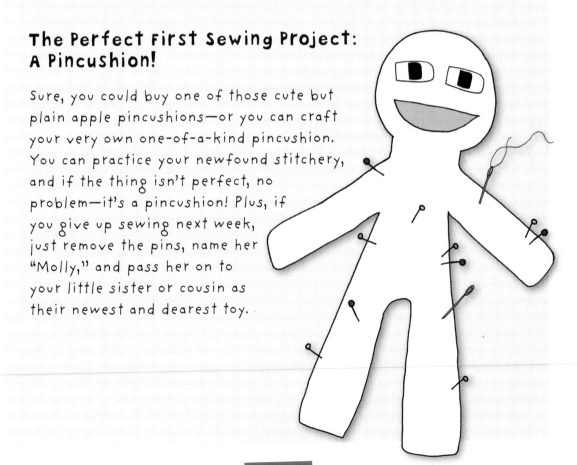

What You Need

- Pillowcase or scrap of fabric

- Needle and thread

- Cotton balls or stuffing material

- Square of felt

- Fabric glue

The HOW-TO

Simply take an old pillowcase or scrap of fabric, fold it in half, and cut out this shape:

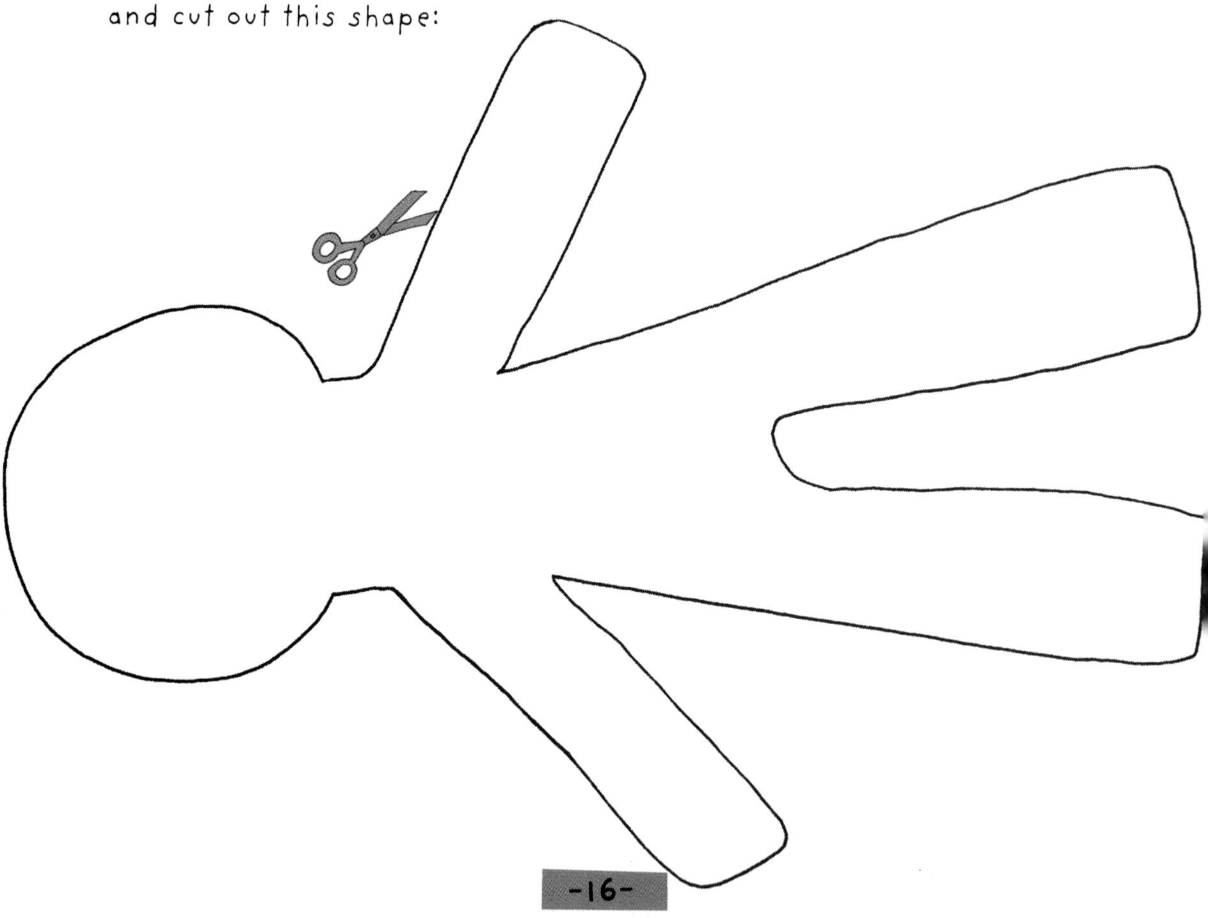

You should now have two pieces of fabric the same size and shape. Before sewing, cut out felt shapes like this:

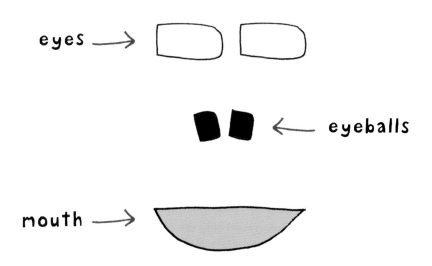

eyes ⟶

eyeballs ⟵

mouth ⟶

These will be the eyes and the mouth. Take a little fabric glue or Steam-A-Seam and glue or iron on a face. Now turn the printed side of the fabric in (the face, too), and start sewing the seam with a backstitch around the head. Work your way around the outside of the body, stopping short of sewing up one of the pincushion's arms and sides. Turn her inside out, stuff her tightly with cotton balls, and finish her off by sewing up the last remaining bits with a hemstitch.

Finito! A cute, utterly unique pincushion. Name her. Love her. Stick her with pins.

CHAPTER FOUR

the tee shirt

- -

A Couple of Words
About the Sacred Tee Shirt

Tee shirts—those comfy, stretchy, cotton wardrobe basics—are
I Wanna Make My Own Clothes money. Most fabrics like woven
cotton, polyester, nylon, and rayon fray when you cut them. But
tee shirts don't fray. They roll and curl on their cut edge, which
can be really annoying if you want to hem them but **really** cool if
you don't! Many of the projects in this book call for cutting into a
tee shirt, lopping off a sleeve, and removing a hem. You could sew
these raw edges, but you'd really need a serger to do a good job.
Instead, I say just cut and let the tee shirt ends roll where they
may. I think it looks cool, if ever so slightly punk rock.

"Whoa, there," you may say.

"What's a serger?" you may ask.

"That sounds foreign and expensive," you may declare.

"And you didn't put that on the list of stuff to buy!"
you may point out.

No need to fret. A serger will give you long-lasting professional
quality, but that's not what we're after, is it? We're looking for

quick and easy ways to make ourselves some new clothes. So for this book: Serger, begone!

But since you asked, a (home-use) serger is usually a little smaller than your average sewing machine, but it uses three to five different threads at the same time. This produces that stitch on the inside of many of our professionally made clothing items that wraps around the edge of a fabric, sort of sealing it (and in this case, making the tee shirt edge behave and not curl). But like I said, we don't need it for any of the duds in this book.

If you breeze through these pages, love making clothes, and want to move on to the next stage with some serious clothing production, a serger is a way cool tool you might consider buying.

Keep It clean!

All of the clothing in this book can be hand washed, no problem, unless otherwise noted. Hanging your clothes on a line to dry will make them last longer (and that goes for all your clothes, not just your homemade ones). But I know—sometimes you've just got to wash it and dry it, machine-style. Use your judgment and understand you're taking a risk. Your clothing could pucker, unravel, or fray. That said, I've washed and dried pretty much all the tees in this book, and they've come out just fine. The edges curl and occasionally they fray, but I think that only adds to the imperfect beauty of my new clothes!

A Map of the Basic Tee Shirt

Here is an illustration of a tee shirt. I've labeled the parts of the shirt here for you so that we have the same vocabulary when it comes to tee shirt construction. That way, if I say, "Cut the left shoulder seam," you'll know exactly what I'm talking about.

neckline

crew neck

shoulder seam

neck seam

armpit

sleeve end or sleeve hem

bottom hem

CHAPTER FIVE

fast no-sew projects

Can't wait another minute? Are you simply aching to start making some new clothes? Then these projects are for you. They require absolutely no sewing, minimal tools, and virtually no doodads. That is, unless you feel like doodadding, in which case I'll point you to the little something-something you can do to make these projects even more singsongy special.

Let's dive right in.

Project #1:
The Deep-V Pin Tee

This shirt can be romantic,
it can be cute, it can be
modern, or it can look
vintage. It all depends on
the pin you choose.

What You Need

- An ordinary tee shirt in your size that has a round crew neck

- A vintage or brand-new brooch* or otherwise ornamental pin

- Scissors

You can find old lapel pins for a dollar at your local thrift store.
Flowers have been a popular motif for brooches throughout the
ages. You could also use a plastic button picturing your favorite
band, but this look would be more rockin' and less lovely. Really,

any kind of pin *would* work—even a safety pin! To make the safety pin look fancy, try weaving a ribbon around the pin part and tying it off with a pretty bow, like so:

The HOW-TO

Lay the tee shirt flat. We're going to remove the ribbed crew neck. Begin cutting straight into the neck on the side, at the shoulder. Then follow the seam that runs around the neck. Do not cut through the front and back at the same time—take the extra minute to go all the way around.

Put the shirt on. Pull down the front of the neck of the newly shirred tee shirt, pinching the front into a V-neck. See how the tee shirt naturally gathers now in the middle, where you're pinching? That's awful pretty. Now put your pin through those gathers and fasten. Voila! Something ordinary is now extraordinary.

✿ brooch \brōch\ n [also broach]:

A grandmotherly word for one of those fancy little pins older ladies like to wear on their lapels, sweater sets, and cocktail dresses. Say it aristocratically while you roll your tongue and laugh out loud.

Project #2:
The Dramatic Shoulder Tee

This is so dang easy, you'll wonder why you didn't think of it before!

What You Need

* An ordinary tee shirt in your size

* Two barrettes with secure closure or two large safety pins or two pieces of cute ribbon

* Scissors

The HOW-TO

Lay the tee shirt flat. Cut off each arm at the seam (cutting the seam off too).

If you're using barrettes, take one and slip the shoulder fabric through like you would a piece of hair and fasten. Repeat on opposite shoulder.

If you choose to do this with safety pins, pinch the shoulder fabric on one shoulder and secure the pin **around** the material (don't put the pin through the fabric, just let it gather in the opening of the pin). Then repeat with the other shoulder.

If ribbon is your tool of choice, simply thread your ribbon through the armhole and tie on the shoulder in a pretty bow. Once again, repeat on opposite shoulder.

The end result? A wildly cute shirt in minutes!

• • • •

Project #3:
The Naughty (Oops, Knotty) Tank Top

You've probably seen these shirts everywhere for big bucks. You can make one in minutes, and it's a great way to use a tee shirt that is cool but just a little too big to wear traditionally.

What You Need

- A tee shirt one to two sizes too big
- Scissors

That's it!

The How-To

Lay the tee shirt flat. Cut off the neck, like you did for the Deep-V Pin Tee (the first project in this chapter), and then cut off each arm at the sleeve seam, like on the Dramatic Shoulder Tee (the second project). Cut the shirt along the shoulder seam.

Slip shirt on. Hold up, or else it will fall off (tee-hee)! Now tie the front and back shoulder pieces together in a knot. Repeat on other shoulder.

Fancy, adorable, and très chichi chic.

● ● ● ●

Project #4: The One-Armed Bandit Tee

Ever heard the words "sophisticated" and "tee shirt" uttered in the same sentence? Now you have!

What You Need

- A tee shirt that fits you very well; snug as a bug in a rug is good, very good

- Scissors

- A ruler

- A pencil

The How-To

Lay the tee shirt flat. Take your ruler and lay it diagonally across the front top of the tee. One end should be at the armpit seam; the other end should be at the opposite side of the neck, just outside the neck seam. Run a pencil along the ruler. You only need to mark the faintest line. Cut through both the front and the back at the same time, along the line, lopping off an arm and the neck as you go. Try the shirt on.

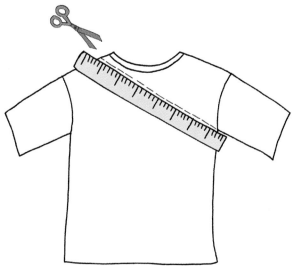

Sophisticated, no? Funky, too!

Alternate Method: You could take this tee a step further, especially if, after trying this shirt on, it doesn't fit quite right. Remove the remaining sleeve. Cut across the shoulder seam. Try shirt on. Tie the single shoulder in a knot, à la Project #3: The Knotty Tank Top.

Still simple and yet oh-so-delightfully cute!

• • • •

Project #5:
The Twisty Turn Halter Tee

This one is slightly trickier
than the others, but it's worth
the extra effort.

What You Need

- A tee shirt two sizes too big for you
- Scissors
- A piece of ribbon about a foot long

The How-To

Lay the tee shirt flat. Cut the neck out, starting on the side and
going all the way around. Cut the sleeves off, like so: Measure
1 inch from the neck at the top of the shoulder and cut an angled
line that ends just under the armpit. Repeat on the other side.

Now, this is where it gets a little complicated. Put the shirt on. It looks ridiculous! Face a mirror. Grab the left shoulder with your right hand and lift it over your head. Now grab the right shoulder with your left hand and lift it over your head.

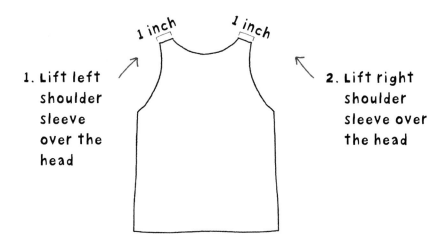

1 inch   1 inch

1. **Lift left shoulder sleeve over the head**

2. **Lift right shoulder sleeve over the head**

Now it looks cute!

Wrap your ribbon around the twisted pieces on your chest, just above your cleavage. Tie a knot. Let excess ribbon hang down freely.

Doodad It

Nab a lifelike but totally fake butterfly from the craft store—the kind that has a small piece of wire attached to the bottom. Wind the wire into the ribbon knot.

Supersimple and superfly!

• • • •

CHAPTER SIX
more tees & shirts

Project #1:
The Boatneck Tee

Only a little bit *Flashdance-esque*, this project is a quick and easy fix for a tee shirt that just fits all wrong.

What You Need

- A tee shirt that fits awkwardly

- Scissors

The HOW-TO

Lay the tee shirt out flat, front facing up. Start at the shoulder seam, 1 1/2 inches to the left of the neck seam, and remove the neck, cutting through both the front and back at the same time. Finish your cut about 1 1/2 inches past the neck seam on the opposite side.

That's it. Now it's more comfortable **and** more exciting!

Doodad It

This is the perfect shirt to doodad. I like adding a felt flower or even a fake "bridal" flower corsage from a craft store to the neck, kind of off-center. You can simply pin it in place with a safety pin. That way, you can remove it when you wash the shirt. You can also change the flower to match your mood and outfit.

● ● ● ●

Project #2:
The Gathers Galore Tee

This one is so tasteful, even your mom will think it's cute. We're just going to add small gathers to the sleeves and front hem of a tee shirt, giving it a little something special but not reworking it in a major way.

- A tee shirt that fits the way you like

- Needle and thread

The HOW-TO

Thread your needle and poke it through the edge of the sleeve hem from the outside (line it up with the shoulder seam). Now do the running man—I mean the running stitch, also known as basting, you may recall. I like to keep the stitches about one third of an inch long. Weave the needle in and out about five or six times before pulling it tight. Then go for another five or six stitches and pull them tight. Go about halfway up the sleeve. When you've gone as far as you're going to go, poke the needle down so that it comes out inside the shirtsleeve. Pull tight and tie in a knot.

You can create a knot by making a stitch on top of your last one, but this time, before you pull the stitch tight, stick the needle through the loop of thread. Pull tight and repeat one more time, and you've got yourself a sturdy little knot.

Repeat this process on the other sleeve and then again at the left or right front-side hem of your tee shirt. When stitching the hem gather, go about 3 to 5 inches straight up toward the neck. Finish with a knot, and you're done.

•   •   •   •

Project #3:
The Deep-V Back Tee

From the front, a very sweet tee shirt. From the back? Wild.

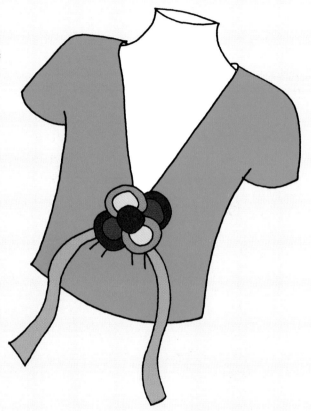

What You Need

- A tee shirt that fits through the shoulders but isn't tight through your torso (aka a "boy cut" tee)

- Tape measure

- Pins

- Scissors

- Needle and thread

- Fake flowers or a patch

- Several 12-inch lengths of ribbon

The HOW-TO

Lay the tee shirt out flat, front facing up. Cut the neck out along the seam, cutting through both the front and back at the same time. Now turn the shirt over so the back is facing up, and make sure it's flat and smooth. Determine the middle of the shirt and how far you want to cut with the tape measure. About 6 inches from the bottom hem is good, but this also depends on the length of the shirt. Mark the shirt's center at the lowest point you want to cut to with a pin. Create an angled line, running your tape

back of shirt

measure from the outside left of the neck to the pin. Cut along the line. Repeat on the right.

Lay the shirt out again flat, the back side facing up. You should now have a large V cut out of the back of the tee shirt. Pinch a piece of fabric on the left side of the bottom point of the V and make a 1-inch fold toward the center and pin. Repeat on the opposite side. Stitch the pleats down with several straight stitches. They don't have to look perfect because in a moment we're going to cover them up. But first, attach a couple of pieces of long ribbon or lace to the stitched area with a few more stitches, letting the length dangle down the back. Finally cover all the stitching with either a couple of faux flowers or a large patch. Sew in place from the inside and knot tightly. Slip on and take a gander at your backside.

Wild!

back of shirt

back of shirt

Project #4:
The Flutter Sleeves Tee

A superquick (like, two-minute) fix for a boring shirt. If you like this look, you could add flutter sleeves to other shirts you've already reconstructed.

What You Need

- Tee shirt
- Scissors

The How-To

Lay the tee shirt flat. Cut along the bottom seam of the sleeve from the outer edge to the armpit. Cut along the top of the sleeve from the edge to the shoulder seam. Make two more cuts, one on each side, approximately 1 inch from this last cut. Slip the tee shirt on.

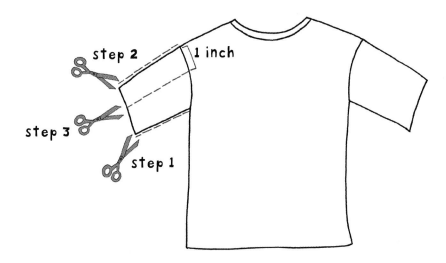

Tie the ends of the two top strips of fabric into a knot on one shoulder. Repeat the whole process on the other arm. Watch your sleeves flutter in the wind!

• • • •

Project #5: The Gathered Shoulders and Flutter Sleeves Tee

This features gathers and flutters, both of which we've covered already, but it produces them together in a slightly different and fabulous way. It's one of my favorite projects. And it's so quick. You'll have a new shirt in fifteen minutes or less!

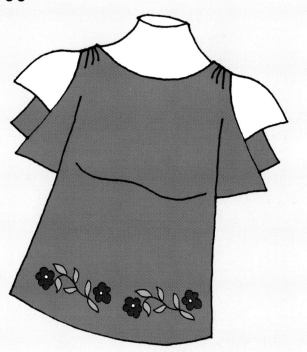

What You Need

- A tee shirt that is two sizes too big
- Needle and thread
- Scissors
- Tape measure

The HOW-TO

Turn the tee shirt inside out and then lay it out flat. We're going to remove the whole top of this shirt. Place the tape measure straight across the front of the shirt, just below the lowest point of the neck. Starting at one sleeve and cutting through both the front and the back at the same time, cut straight across, following the line of the tape measure.

Now that we've split the top of the shirt wide open, we want to put it back together. Keep it inside out. Take your needle and thread and, starting at the outside shoulder seam of the tee, sew a running stitch 4 inches toward where the neck used to be. Pull tight, gathering the shoulder up into pretty neat bunches, and tie a knot. Repeat on the other shoulder. You need to make sure you leave enough open, unsewn space for your head, so pay attention and make sure to leave room.

Beautiful! The shoulders are pronounced with their sweet little gathers, and because we didn't stitch the sleeves back together, they flutter sweetly in the wind.

Alternate Method: If you have a shirt that is only slightly big but you still want to make this tee, try this: Instead of lopping off the tee from the neck up, simply cut along the top shoulder seam, starting at the sleeve end and moving the scissors all the way to the neck. Repeat on the other side. Cut along the neck seam to remove the neck. Then follow the same directions as above, only reducing the 4-inch-long running stitch to 2.

● ● ● ●

Project #6: The Zany Zipper Tee

Keep your eyes peeled at the thrift shops, and you'll no doubt spot some old zippers, still in the packages, never used, for ten or twenty cents apiece. Look for bright and vibrant sherbet-type colors, but classic black is good too. Or pick up a few at the local sewing shop for a couple of bucks each.

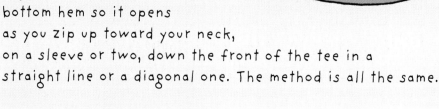

You can put a zipper anywhere—at the bottom hem so it opens as you zip up toward your neck, on a sleeve or two, down the front of the tee in a straight line or a diagonal one. The method is all the same.

What You Need

- A tee shirt that fits you nicely

- A zipper or two in colors that match the shirt

- Pins

- Scissors

- Needle and thread or embroidery floss in a contrasting or matching color

The HOW-TO

Figure out where you want the zipper. The top of the zipper needs to be on an edge of the tee shirt. Once you've figured out where it's going to go, pin it down on top of the tee very carefully along both of the outer edges, making sure not to interfere with the zipper itself. Try to keep it as flat as possible, and make sure you pin through only one layer of fabric.

Once it's completely secure, slowly unzip the zipper. Take your scissors and cut along the zipper line. Slowly zip it back up. Then sew the zipper in place with a straight stitch, using either thread and small stitches (for a subtle look) or embroidery floss and larger stitches (for a bold finish). Stick to the outer edges of the zipper placket, and you won't have trouble zipping and unzipping when you're all done. Knot your thread or floss when you've finished, sewing your last stitches on the inside of the tee shirt.

Slip on and unzip slightly for a daring, darling, punk rock look!

•   •   •   •

Project #7:
The Scrabble Tee

Want a tee shirt that says something? Got a lot to say? This shirt is for you. And it also makes the greatest gift.

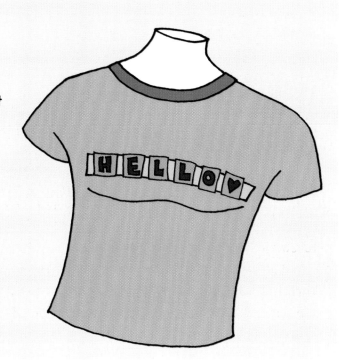

What You Need

- A plain tee shirt that fits well

- 1 to 2 yards of 1- to 2-inch-wide Velcro (stick-on is best) in a light or bright color (no black)

- A hefty needle and thread

- Black permanent marker, like a Sharpie

- 3/4-inch-tall alphabet stencils

- Scissors

The How-To

Velcro comes in rolls or strips or tabs and includes two parts that stick together miraculously. The softer, fuzzy piece is often referred to as the "female," and the prickly part the "male." The reverse side of both pieces is smooth and flat and stiff.

Measure and cut an approximately 10-inch-long strip of only the fuzzy female side of your Velcro. You want it as long as needed to comfortably cross the front of the tee shirt without wrapping under the arms. Sew this female strip of Velcro (fuzzy side facing out) to the chest of the shirt straight across horizontally. Velcro is a little hard to sew on because it is made of a very tough fabric; a thicker needle will help.

Now we'll create the letters. Cut a long strip of "male" Velcro. Place an **A** stencil over the strip (you'll be using the stencils on the smooth "back" side of the Velcro) and color in the letter with your permanent marker. Leaving about an inch between letters, move the stencil down and color in a **B** and so on until you've covered the whole alphabet. You will probably want to make double or even triple stencils of all your vowels and common letters like **D, G, H, L, M, N, P, R, S,** and **T.**

Now the shirt is your paper, and the Velcro "tiles" let you express your ever-changing moods! One day you can spell out your name; another day, your love for a particular band. . . . Whatever you want to say (within reason) is possible. Change your phrases weekly, daily, even moment to moment.

Doodad It

If you're giving this stupendous tee shirt/game as a gift, why not make a little drawstring bag for the letter tiles? Use any scrap fabric you have lying around. You'll need two pieces, each about 8 inches by 8 inches (give or take an inch or two). Place the pieces of fabric on top of each other, right sides facing in. Sew along the outer edge on three sides with a basic straight stitch or a backstitch, whichever you're most comfortable with. But leave an inch open on the two sides near the top opening.

Turn your bag right side out. Fold down the top edge of the bag inward, about three quarters of an inch. Pin down, then sew, taking extra care to stay as close to the bottom hem as possible. You are creating a "tunnel" for the drawstring at the top of your bag.

When you're finished making the tunnel, attach a safety pin to one end of a thin piece of ribbon, close it, and feed it through all the way until it pokes back out where you started. Remove the safety pin. Fill your bag with tiles and pull the ribbon tight. Tie in a pretty bow.

You could also take that safety pin you used to push the ribbon through and attach the new bag, filled with the tiles, to the hem of the shirt so your friend (or, face it, you) will never lose your ABC's.

●　●　●　●

Project #8:
The '80s-Style Off-the-Shoulder Tee

Hate the 1980s? Don't like
the off-the-shoulder look?
Don't worry, when worn
"normal," this tee has
a superhip cowl-neck.
Oh, and take your time
sewing, because the
stitches will show.

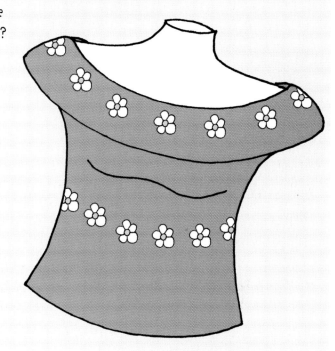

What You Need

* A long tee shirt in your size

* Scissors

* Needle and matching thread

* Pins

The HOW-TO

Cut off each of the sleeves at an angle, starting at the armpit and angling toward the outer seam of the neckline. Then cut straight across, through both layers of fabric, from sleeve to sleeve just under the neckline, cutting the neck off. Cut a 4- to 6-inch strip off the bottom hem.

Lay the tee shirt flat, front side facing up. Take the bottom hem you just cut off and position it horizontally across the top of the shirt. Take the front top off the shirt and place it inside the hem strip, centered horizontally. Pin in place and flip over, then do the same on the back side. There should now be a hole between the original shirt and the new strip on each side for your arms and one large hole for your head.

Sew along the front top of the shirt, where you pinned, with a hemstitch. The stitching will show, so take your time and try to make evenly spaced, small stitches. Repeat on the back. Slip the shirt on and poke your arms through the holes on each side. Pull the hem strip down on your shoulders. Voila—one very hip, '80s-style, off-the-shoulder tee! Or leave the hem strip up on your shoulders and note how your cute cowl-neck drapes elegantly.

• • • •

Project #9: The Lace Cap Sleeves Tee

One of the biggest problems I often have with tee shirts that I pick up at the secondhand stores is the fit of the arm, or the cut of the sleeve. They are either too big or too tight—never just right. Lace is a quick fix for that problem, and it adds a new dimension to a tee shirt, taking it from ho-hum to stylin' sweet.

What You Need

- A tee shirt that isn't particularly exciting—perhaps it has icky sleeves, but otherwise, it fits fine

- 3 feet of 1 1/2-inch- to 3-inch-wide lace (at least one edge of the lace should be straight)

- Needle and thread

- Pins

- Scissors

- Tape measure

The How-To

Remove the sleeves at a slight angle, cutting from armpit to shoulder seam, leaving approximately 3 to 4 inches of shoulder width on each side.

Measure around the circumference of the sleeve, then cut a piece of lace that length. Pin the straight edge of the lace to the cut edge of your tee shirt (lace on top of tee). Fold the lace under as you get closer to the armpit, tapering it as you go. Once it's completely pinned, turn the shirt inside out and sew along the edge using a straight stitch (make sure to use thread that matches the color of the lace). Repeat on the other arm.

Lace + tee shirt = fancy new shirt!

Doodad It

Does the shirt need something else? Then let's add a gathered V-neck!

Remove the neck of the shirt, cutting along the outer edge of the neck seam. In front, cut a slight V-neck. Take your needle and thread—this time a color that matches the tee shirt—and starting at the top of the V-neck, make a running stitch that runs vertically toward the bottom of the shirt—just about 2 inches long. Your last stitch should sit on the inside of the tee. Pull tight and knot.

You can even do the same thing at the side hems of the shirt. Starting at the left bottom hem, make a vertical running stitch upward, approximately 4 to 5 inches long. End on the inside of the tee. Pull tight and knot. Repeat on the right side.

More gathers = more cuteness!

• • • •

Project #10:
The Pillowcase Empire-Waist Shirt

Very simple, and actually quite flattering, this shirt is a mighty fine use for a pillowcase that is adorably cute but just doesn't match the décor of your room.

What You Need

- A pillowcase that is wide enough for you to wear as a shirt

- Needle and thread

- Scissors

- 5 feet of 3-inch-wide binding tape, with lace or fancy trim

- Steam-A-Seam or some other paper-backed fusible web tape

The How-To

Lay the pillowcase flat. Cutting through both sides of the pillowcase, slice a centered 9-inch-long, 1/4-inch-deep hole on the seam on the short end of the case that's been sewed shut. This is for your neck.

From the center of that last cut, cut down for 5 1/2 inches. Fold the flaps you've just created inward, creating a V-neckline. Iron these down and secure them in place with fusible web tape.

Cut approximately 6 1/2-inch angled cuts to the left and right of your V-neck. Think halter top. These are for the arms. Try the shirt on at this point and make sure it fits. Adjust accordingly.

Fold the arm seams inward half an inch, then iron them down with more fusible web tape.

You want this shirt to hit at midhip, give or take a couple of inches, so if you need to trim the bottom, try on the shirt first and mark where you want to cut. Before hemming, add a four-inch slit to each side. Hem all your raw edges with more fusible web tape.

Slip the shirt back on. We're going to add the binding (fabric folded into a neat strip and sold on a roll or card) to give it a cute

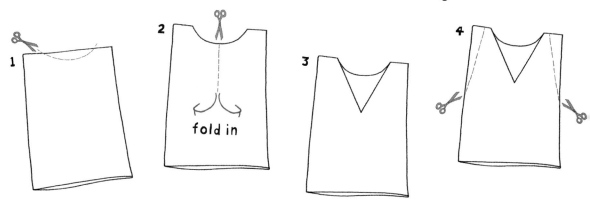

1

2

fold in

3

4

shape. The goal is to create a classic empire waist—the style often thought of when one speaks of "baby doll dresses." Essentially, it's a cinched high waist. With the shirt on, hold up the binding, centering it in front of you. Place it on your upper stomach, an inch or two below your chest, and tie it in back. Mess with the placement until it's exactly where you like it. Pin it in place just once in the front, once on the left, and once on the right. Untie the back and take the shirt off.

Lay the pillowcase flat and, with a washable marker or a pencil, make a light mark on the top edge of the binding and the bottom edge, both on the right and left, near your pins. Remove the pins, but keep them nearby. Cinch two tiny little vertical pleats on each side where you made those marks, maybe half an inch. This will create shape where there was none. Hold the pleats steady, then line up your binding over the marks (and over the pleats) and pin in place.

Now all you need to do is stitch down the binding in the two places where you made the pleats. You can even do this with contrasting thread. Sew cute little X's instead of an ordinary straight stitch. Slip on your new frock, tie the binding in back, and dance around and around.

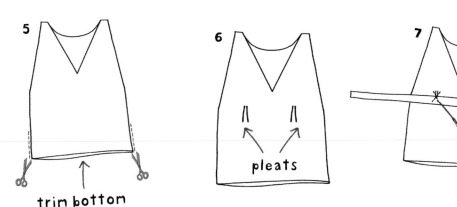

5

trim bottom
if necessary

6

pleats

7

CHAPTER SEVEN

tanks & halters

Project #1:
The Simple Beaded Pin Tank

Here is another ridiculously simple but stylish shirt that, when finished, looks equally good with skirts or with jeans.

What You Need

- A tee shirt in your size

- Two or more large, 1 1/2-inch-long safety pins, shiny gold or silver in color

- A handful of beads

The How-To

Lay the tee shirt flat. Cut off the sleeves. Remove the neck, taking your time and going all the way around.

Thread a few beads on to the point of a safety pin, then wrap the pin around one of the shoulders so that the beads are showing. Fasten it, taking care not to pinch or poke any of the fabric. Pull the pin down vertically toward the armpit area. Repeat on the other side.

Doodad It

For an even fancier look, add more beaded pins on top of the original pins.

•　•　•　•

Project #2:
The Ribbon Tank

This involves some sewing, but it's worth the time. You'll turn a sporty tee into a flirtatious summer top!

What You Need

- A tee shirt that is just slightly big

- Needle and thread

- Scissors

- Pins

- 2 yards of 1/4-inch- to 3/4-inch-wide ribbon or lace (something that looks good on both sides)

- Large safety pin

The HOW-TO

Cut an angled line from one armpit to the outer neck seam, cutting through both the front and the back of the shirt at the same time. Repeat on the other sleeve. Make your last cut through both layers of fabric horizontally, just below the neckline, removing the neck of the shirt entirely. Fold about 1 inch of the fabric in front inward and pin it in place. Sew a straight stitch along the bottom edge of the fold, being careful to maintain a tunnel of fabric for the ribbon to squeak through. Repeat this process on the back side. Now you have a tube in both the front and the back.

Take your ribbon or lace and attach a safety pin to one end. Close the pin. Carefully feed the pin through the tube in front and around again through the tube in back until the ends of the ribbon or lace meet on a shoulder. Tie into a pretty bow. Put it on and adjust, pulling the ribbon tighter or looser depending upon your desired fit. Retie and let the excess ribbon fall romantically down one side.

Marvel at your newfound sewing skills!

Doodad It

After you've finished, you can easily swap the ribbon or lace you use, effortlessly changing the look of the shirt from one wear to the next. You could even double up and have two contrasting colors of lace or ribbon (provided they're narrow enough to both fit through the neck tube at the same time). Pin the two pieces of lace or ribbon together and feed them at once.

● ● ● ●

Project #3:
The Scarf Shoulder Big Ol' Bow Tank

This is very couture-looking, very chichi, very cute, and very simple.

What You Need

- A tank top (or tee shirt with the arms cut off)
- A long scarf (not the square kind)
- Needle and thread

The HOW-TO

Slice one shoulder open at the shoulder seam. You now have a front strap and a back strap. Fold the scarf in half lengthwise and cut in half. Sew the cut edge of one of the scarf pieces to the end of the back strap. If it's wider than the tank strap, simply gather or make small folds till it is approximately the same width. Repeat with the other piece of scarf, sewing it to the end of the front strap. Slip on. Tie the scarf into a giant bow. Or tie it into a large knot and let the scarf ends dangle toward the floor dramatically.

Take a gander in a mirror and delight in your very expensive-looking, new, designer tank!

Doodad It

Go the extra mile and do up the other shoulder with a contrasting scarf.

• • • •

Project #4: The Scarf Halter Top

You could simply take a square scarf, fold it in half diagonally so that it's a triangle, and tie it on, effortlessly transforming a throwaway accessory into a glamorous shirt. But by taking one extra step, you create "fashion."

What You Need

- A sizable square scarf

- A 2-foot piece of wide ribbon or a second scarf

- A 1-inch-by-2-inch piece of fusible web tape

- An O-ring—you can use anything that's about 1 to 3 inches in diameter; it should be fairly flat and either plastic, wood, or metal, like a key ring, shower curtain ring, purse piece, belt buckle, plumbing fixture, or binder ring (the latter is cheap and easy to find at your local office supply store).

The HOW-TO

Fold the scarf in half diagonally so that it forms a triangle. Fold just the top point of the scarf through the O-ring and secure it around the ring with fusible web tape. Iron on and make sure you have a good seal. Feed the wide ribbon or second scarf through the O-ring and tie it around your neck. Bring the bottom two points of your original scarf triangle around your upper waist and tie.

End result? A supercute and extra-chic halter top that looks like you spent big cash.

● ● ● ●

Project #5:
Bathing Suit/Halter Top Numero Uno

For this item we're essentially taking an unused, unpopular tee shirt and opening up all the seams so that it is an awkwardly shaped but otherwise flat piece of stretchy material. And then we're making a funky shape out of said material. It's in fact so easy that it may inspire you to cut up more tees and come up with your own shapes that could, with a nip and a tuck, become an entirely new shirt. This tee starts out its life as ordinary, but once it meets you, it becomes something so very, very extraordinary.

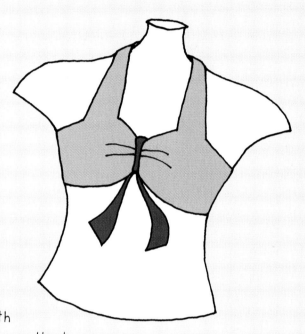

What You Need

- A tee shirt that is anywhere from one to four sizes too big

- Needle and a short length of thread

- A 3-inch piece of coordinating ribbon

The HOW-TO

Lay the tee shirt flat. Cut off the arms at the seams. Turn the shirt over so the back is facing up. Slice the back open in a straight line from the center back neck to center back hem. Turn shirt over again so the front is now facing up, and open the shirt up, laying it out flat on the floor.

Take a look at the illustration below. You want to cut out this shape. Cut the silhouette thick, as pictured, because the edges can curl in if it's too big. You can't affix material if the bikini top is too small.

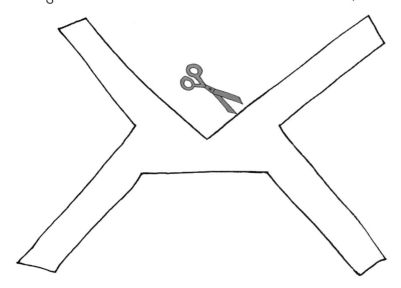

Now try it on and adjust it. The bottom long pieces tie around your back. The upper long pieces tie around your neck. Pinch the center front together and tie the ribbon around and into a small bow or knot.

Wear with your bikini bottoms. Wear with cute board shorts. Wear with a mini skirt. Wear it under a flowing top. You can wear this wherever you want, but trust me, you will want to wear it!

● ● ● ●

Project #6:
The Bandeau Bathing Top

This is a great use for a cool shirt that has been struck with the dreaded pit stains!

What You Need

- A tee shirt, the bigger the better
- An O-ring (see Project #4: The Scarf Halter Top for explanation)
- Scissors
- Needle and thread

The HOW-TO

Lay the tee shirt flat. Cut a straight line across the tee shirt from one underarm to the other. You can and should cut through both the front and the back at the same time. Measure down 5 inches. Cut across the shirt in another straight line, again through both the front and the back at the same time. Put this small tube of tee shirt to the side.

Now you should still have a sizable hem. Measure from the cut edge down 5 inches and cut your last straight line across the tee shirt, cutting through the front and back at the same time. Now you have two pieces that are the same size. Open each piece up by cutting a straight line across the shorter end, at the seam.

Poke one end of the first piece through your O-ring and pull it through till the ends meet. Stitch them together with a straight stitch. Take the second piece and poke it through the O-ring and pull it through in the other direction till the ends meet. Stitch them together as well.

Straighten out the tee shirt pieces, making them as flat as can be, and then tie the ends around your back. Straighten and fuss with it until it comfortably covers your chest.

Don at the beach with some shorts or under a button-down shirt with a cute skirt. Hooray for DIY beachwear!

• • • •

Project #7:
The Marilyn Halter Tee

This is the perfect antidote to a boring ol' tee. It's a great summer basic with a retro feel. Choose a plain shirt or one with a graphic. Either way, the end result will be much more exciting than the original.

What You Need

- A tee shirt in your size

- Scissors

The How-To

Lay the tee shirt flat and start by cutting off the sleeves at the seams. Remove the neckband, too. Turn the tee shirt over and cut straight across from armpit to armpit **in the back only**. Turn the tee back over, so the front is facing up, pulling the back shoulder piece you just cut straight up and flat. Cut a vertical line from the back of the neck, straight up.

You now have two long pieces that will form the ties that wrap around your neck. Trim these pieces so they are straight and slim. Slip shirt on and tie the straps around your neck.

Go knock on your neighbor's door and show off your latest, loveliest creation! Go on, go!

Doodad It

Take a 4-inch piece of ribbon and knot it on to the base of the neck strap on one side. Repeat on the other side. This will make the neckline pull straight, for a very retro, fifties look.

● ● ● ●

Project #8:
The Open-Back Tube Top

This is just fun. Pure fun. And so simple. The only catch? You need a friend to help you into it.

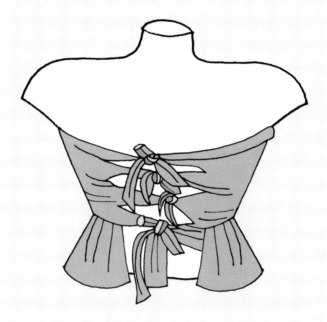

What You Need

- A tee shirt slightly larger than you would normally wear

- Scissors

The How-To

Lay the tee shirt flat and cut straight across from armpit to armpit, cutting off the neck and sleeves. What you're left with is a large tube, and the opening is hemmed on one side. Lay it out flat with the back side facing up. Being careful not to cut the front, poke your scissor blade 1 inch from the top of your tube on one side. Put your scissors in the hole and cut from one side seam to the other, straight across. Do this again 1 inch below that slash. Repeat at least two more times or until you get to about 1 inch above the bottom hem.

Now with the shirt laid out flat and the slash cuts facing up, make a vertical cut that crosses all your slashes straight down the center.

front

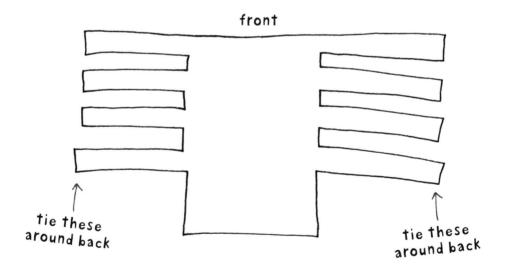

tie these
around back

tie these
around back

Now get that much-needed friend. Hold the front of the shirt up to your torso. Have your buddy tie the strips in the back into knotted bows, pulling tightly to fit the top to your body perfectly.

Once the shirt is tied into its bows, you should be able to slip it on and off without your kind friend's assistance.

This tube top is so cute (and easy), your friend will ask you to make one for her next! Go ahead, it takes just minutes.

Doodad It

Turn the shirt over so that the front is now facing up. Measure down 2 1/2 inches from the center top of the tube. Poke your scissor through the shirt and then cut out a small 1/2-inch circle. Take a short piece of ribbon or lace and feed it through the hole and up around the top of the shirt, tying it into a pretty little knot in front. This adds a nice detail in front so that the tube top isn't just plain and ordinary in front. Change the ribbon to match whatever pants, skirt, or shorts you're wearing.

●　●　●　●

CHAPTER EIGHT
jackets & sweaters

Project #1: The Incredibly Expensive-Looking, Beguilingly Romantic Sweater

Take a gander in an Anthropologie (a cool store that people like Julia Roberts shop in), and you'll see a dozen sweaters that look like this one. Sweet, vintage-inspired, and incredibly romantic, this sweater starts out as a plain-Jane cardigan, a humble castoff from your closet or neighborhood thrift store.

What You Need

- A plain cardigan in your size (or close to your size)
- Scissors

- Needle and thread

- Various ribbons

- New buttons

The HOW-TO

Lay the sweater flat. Cut one sleeve off a couple of inches below the elbow. Repeat on the other arm. Fold sleeve hem edges inward on the first arm and pin in place. Repeat on the other sleeve. Sew the new hem in place with a hemstitch. Repeat on the other sleeve.

Now measure and cut a length of ribbon to wrap around the new "cuff." Cut another piece the same length. Wrap the ribbon around the cuff so that it covers your hem stitching. Pin in place. Using thread that matches the color of your ribbon, sew in place using small straight stitches.

Remove the buttons on the cardigan with your seam ripper or a small pair of scissors. Cut another piece of ribbon 1 inch longer than the button placket. This ribbon can match the ribbon on your sleeves, or it can be contrasting, for a funkier look. Place it over the placket so that half an inch extends beyond the sweater at both the top and bottom. Fold the ends under and pin the ribbon in place. Sew the ribbon down, using thread that is the same color as the ribbon.

Replace the buttons you took off earlier, or reattach completely new buttons where the old ones used to be. If you can't tell where the buttons once were, line up the buttonhole placket with your newly adorned ribbon placket, and you'll be able to tell exactly where to sew your new or old buttons.

Pretty, pretty!

Doodad It

You've now covered the basics. You could stop there...or you could continue to embellish and beautify your new "vintage" sweater. Sew on a random piece of trim or ribbon over one shoulder. Sew a fake or handmade fabric flower on the chest. Iron patches on to the elbows. You could even sew on a "pocket" by cutting a piece of fabric into a square and stitching three sides to the sweater, leaving the top hem open.

● ● ● ●

Don't throw away those sweater cuffs!

You can wear them as is with a tee shirt for a funky art-school cuff look, or you can make 'em into mittens! Turn the cuffs inside out and make a 3-inch-long cut perpendicular to the cuff's edge, just 1 inch from the cuff's side seam (for the thumb, silly!). Close up the cut seams with a backstitch. Turn them right side out, and you've got groovy new mittens. Add flowers and ribbons to beautify.

Project #2:
The Fur-Trimmed Hoodie Sweatshirt

I got this idea from a cute boy I spotted one day wearing a sweatshirt just like this. Perhaps not the most masculine look, but I have to say, he and the sweatshirt looked pretty studly.

What You Need

- A hooded sweatshirt, either a pullover or the zip-up type

- Feather boa (these are sold at every craft and fabric store, as well as at many dollar stores)

- Needle and thread (color should match the shade of the feathers)

The How-To

It's pretty simple. Start at one end of the hood and pin the boa along the edge. When you get to the other end of the hood, cut off the extra boa. Sew it in place with delicate "hidden" stitches. The only downside to this cute, quick makeover? Your sweatshirt is no longer entirely washable. Spot clean this one only, and be careful to avoid the feathers.

Alternate Method: You could also make a fur-trimmed vest. Try cutting off the sleeves of a sweatshirt or sweater or even a jean jacket. Then sew pieces of fur or feather boa to the armholes for a frisky, fun vest.

Either way, a little faux fur or feather makes any item fantastically more fun.

Doodad It

With the leftover boa, trim any pockets the sweatshirt might also be sporting. Or better yet, sew a strip of boa all the way around the arm sleeve (where the sleeve connects to the sweatshirt) for a cool Arctic-cutie look.

●　●　●　●

Project #3:
The Jean Jacket Sweater

Part jean jacket, part sweater,
this project will result in a
one-of-a-kind sweater
that no one but you will own.

What You Need

- A pair of jeans you no longer want; they should have a button waistband and back pockets

- A basic sweater—a zip front is ideal, but a button front will work as well

- Needle and thread

- Pins

- Scissors

- Seam ripper

The How-To

Let's start by destroying that pair of jeans. I actually went out and purchased a pair of cheap jeans at the thrift store for this project because I wasn't comfortable ripping apart any pants I once wore!

Remove the waistband of the jeans with a seam ripper and/or pair of small scissors. This is harder than it sounds. Just take your time because you want most of the waistband intact. If you destroy part of it while removing it, though, it's not the end of the world. We won't be using the back of the waistband, so I suggest starting back there and working your way to the front, since you'll probably get better at it as you go. I had to remove the bottom seam of my belt loops to get the waistband off, but I just reattached them later and it was no problem, so don't worry if the same happens to you.

Once you've removed the waistband successfully, breathe a sigh of relief. The hardest part is over!

Now remove the back pockets. Usually you just have to get the first couple of stitches out of one of the seams on the upper corners and they'll rip right off with minimal force. You could sew these pockets to anything for instant pocket action! You could try them on a tee shirt or a purse, or they can become part of a wall organizer for your room or car. But right now we want to attach them to our sweater.

Place them on the front of the sweater, one on each side of the button placket. You can place them high on the chest or lower, at the waist. That's where I like them best. But pin them on and slip into that sweater and see where they work best for you.

Once you've pinned them in place, sew the pockets to the sweater on three sides, leaving them open at the top and completely functional. Now is the time to nab that thimble if you have one. Protect those fingers. I like to sew the pockets on with the same color thread that was on the jeans in the first place, which in most cases is a warm gold. But you can sew them on with a dark denim blue color or, if you're feeling wild, a contrasting color thread. Even thick embroidery thread would work here. Take your time— denim is a little thicker than your average fabric, and sometimes it's work to get the needle through two layers. But if you go slow, it will all work out in the end.

Back to the waistband. Size up the neck of your sweater. Is it big and bulky? Then you'll need to remove it. Is it dainty and unassuming, narrower than the denim waistband? Then you can leave it in place and sew right on top of it. If you have to remove the neck of the sweater, try to do it just above the neck seam. This leaves a little something-something to sew your waistband to, so that it can become the new neckband!

Button your jean waistband. Button up your sweater. Center that old waistband button over the top of the button placket of your sweater. Pin it to the neck, starting at the center front. When you get to the back, you can trim off any excess and stitch the end seams down as well.

Now unbutton the waistband's button. Your waistband will extend farther than the neck in front because of the way we centered the button. That's okay—it gives your sweater a cool motorcycle-jacket vibe. Now, if you're stitching the jean waistband to an existing neckline, you may need to sew both the bottom and the top edge of the old waistband. If you're sewing this to a sweater that had the neck removed, you'll sew only the bottom edge.

Sweet, no?

Doodad It

To really finish this sweater off right, you can trim out the inside of the neck. A piece of felt works great for this or even a strip of 3/4-inch-wide binding. Open the sweater up and cut a strip of felt or binding that will cover the inner neck of your new sweater. You can iron this on with fusible web or sew it in place with a light straight stitch, taking care not to poke your needle through the outer layer of denim. If you choose a bright color, it will add style to the unbuttoned sweater as well as functionality.

And don't throw away the rest of those jeans. Denim scraps will come in handy for patches and trim on future projects.

●　●　●　●

Project #4: The Baby Blanket Shawl

You know those cute
knit ponchos that cost
mountains of money?
You can make one. No
crocheting necessary.

What You Need

- Square baby blanket (check the good ol' thrift stores, they have oodles of these things)

- Scissors

- 2 feet of 1- to 2-inch-wide ribbon

- Tape measure

- Needle and thread

The HOW-TO

Fold the blanket diagonally in half into a triangle. Measure the length of the fold so you can find the center. From the center point, cut a straight line along the fold, 5 inches in each direction. Slip it on over your head.

Cut the ribbon into two 10-inch pieces. Take one piece and fold it over the front slit you cut for your head. Pin down and then sew with a classic straight stitch. Repeat with the other piece of ribbon on the back slit. Press the trim with an iron for a nice, clean fold. This will keep the cut blanket edges from fraying and will make it look oh-so-modern as well!

Shockingly cute for an old baby blanket, don't you think?

Doodad It

You can usually pick up large fuzzy yarn or furry pom-poms at most craft stores. Buy four pom-poms and sew one to each point of the baby blanket for a fun, fancy finish.

• • • •

CHAPTER NINE

skirts

Project #1:
The Tee Shirt Skirt

Honestly, this may be the cutest thing in this book. And can we say "easy"?

What You Need

- A tee shirt that is about as wide as your hips (just hold it up by the underarms and then measure it against your hips)

- Needle and thread

- Tape measure

- Scissors

The HOW-TO

Lay the tee shirt flat. Cut off one arm—just one. Lay the tape measure across the shirt so that it's parallel with the shoulders. Line it up just under the neckline. Cut a straight line that cuts off the shoulders, neck, and the top half of the remaining arm.

Turn the shirt inside out. Sew up the hole left by the first arm you cut off, trying to keep a straight line from the side seam of the shirt. Do this with a simple backstitch.

Turn the tee shirt right side out and lay it out flat again. You want to slice along the underarm seam of the sleeve, stopping when you get to the body of the shirt.

Slip the tee shirt on like a skirt. The arm that is now sliced into two pieces becomes the side tie. Make a knot, pulling it in a little at the waist.

This is especially cute if you have a shirt that bears an emblem, logo, or saying and you turn the printed side of the tee around to your bum.

Doodad It

Lace it up! Turn the skirt inside out. Stick a long strip of fusible web tape along the bottom. Remove the top paper and stick a wide piece of lace on top so that it hangs out from the bottom of the skirt. Iron down gently and turn right side out. Voila! Speedy lace trim!

● ● ● ●

Project #2:
The Beach Cover-Up Tee Skirt

Really, this is just a shorter, quicker variation on the previous project, the Tee Shirt Skirt. Here we turn a smaller, shorter tee into a beach mini: the perfect poolside cover. How long will it take? About a minute, maybe two. That's it!

What You Need

* A tee shirt—short and sassy is fine, but it should be wide enough to fit snugly on your hips

* Needle and thread

* Scissors

The HOW-TO

Cut straight across from armpit to armpit, hacking off the sleeves and neck as you go. The top will roll slightly. Slip on over your suit and roll down the "waist" to your liking.

More do-it-yourself beachwear. The summer has never been more economically adorable!

• • • •

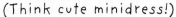

Project #3:
A Most Mighty Mini

This is a classic. Gals have been making these for years. The same method will work on your jeans, trousers, corduroys, khakis, whatever. But don't stop there. This will even work with overalls. (Think cute minidress!)

What You Need

- A pair of pants that fit you nicely in the waist, but not a pair you care for so much

- Pins

- Scissors

- Seam ripper or small scissors

- Needle and thread

- A patch (optional but handy)

The HOW-TO

Cut the pants off several inches below where you want your skirt to fall. Rip out the inner thigh seams on both legs with your seam ripper or small scissors. Once you've ripped apart about 2 inches, you can pull firmly and split the seams in an instant. You'll still have to go back and rip the crotch seams out too.

Slip your ripped pants on. I advise doing this before pinning or sewing so you can see how the lines of the new skirt will fall. Every type of pant is different, and while the basic construction is similar, different-length inseams will result in slightly different-shaped skirts.

Take off the ripped pants and lay them out on the floor. You'll be able to fold over that extra flap of material—see the part I mean?—to make up for the gap on either the front or the back.

You may need to cut a triangle of fabric from the leg to make up for the gap on the opposite side, but this depends on how short you desire your skirt. If you're making a micromini, no triangle will be necessary. But if you're making a knee-length number, you'll likely need that extra smidge of fabric.

Pin the seams in place, forming a cute miniskirt. Try the skirt back on. Adjust any ill-fitting seams. Mark with a pin where you'd like the skirt to hit on your legs. If you want to hem the bottom with a simple hemstitch, then leave yourself an extra inch on the bottom. If, like me, you want to let the hem fray, cut it off one eighth of an inch longer than where you want it (to allow for a small amount of unraveling). Remove the skirt and cut it to the desired length. Try it on again. Readjust any pins for the last time before sewing up the seams.

Remove the skirt, turn it inside out, and sew up all your pinned seams with a sturdy backstitch.

When you're working with jeans or any other heavy fabric, you may get a little "poof" or buckle in the fabric that is unsightly. This often happens where the old crotch of the pants meets the front or back of your new skirt; it happens even to the best seamstresses. That's what the optional patch is for. Just cover the poof or buckle with a cool patch. It makes the skirt more interesting, more unique, and it covers up any easy-to-make mistakes.

Doodad It

Add lace to the underside of the skirt so it peeks out the bottom (see Project #1: The Tee Shirt Skirt earlier in this chapter). Add more patches. Add rickrack (that squiggly-line trim that is so gosh-darn cute) to the hem. Affix iron-on letters along the hem, proclaiming I MADE THIS or I LOVE ETHAN or announcing your professional wrestling pseudonym. Mine's "Super-Clea."

●　●　●　●

Project #4:
The Pleated Miniskirt

This is a relatively easy skirt to make that can look pretty or funky depending upon the fabric you choose. It takes some time, but it's worth it. You cannot make this skirt without an iron.

- A flat sheet or 2 to 3 yards of cotton fabric

- Iron

- Lots of pins

- Needle and thread

- Tape measure

- Scrap tee shirt hem (4 to 6 inches in height—take from a tee shirt that doesn't fit well or that you don't wear)

- Steam-A-Seam or other fusible web tape

The How-To

Measure around your hips at their widest point. Mark this measurement down on a piece of paper. You'll need it in a minute.

Lay out the fabric or sheet so it's flat and smooth. Cut one long strip that is at least 2 yards long and approximately 10 inches wide. Now we need to hem one long side of the strip. You can do this effortlessly with your iron and some Steam-A-Seam or other fusible web tape. Take your time and make the hem straight and even.

Keep the iron on. With your fabric laid out flat, we're going to iron folds, or pleats, into the "skirt." This is where the tape measure comes in. Take the fabric and create each pleat by folding 1 inch of the fabric over onto itself at a time. If you have lots of fabric (more than 2 yards), you can space the pleats quite close together—say, at 1-inch increments. If you have less fabric, space the pleats farther apart—about 2 to 2 1/2 inches. Once you fold over the fabric, iron the pleat down carefully and then pin the pleat at the top edge (the edge of the fabric or sheet that you didn't hem). Continue doing this until you have pleated the whole strip of fabric, measuring the length of fabric as you go and adjusting the size of the pleats. You want your final result to equal that number you wrote down.

When you're all done pleating and pinning and the fabric is the right length (to properly wrap around your hips), stitch your pleats down with a straight stitch at the top edge. Now pin the short ends of the fabric together to form a tube. This is the body of the skirt. Sew or iron this seam together with fusible web hem tape. Set aside the pleated "skirt" for a moment.

Slip the cutoff tee shirt hem around your waist. If it's too big, take in the side hem so it rests on your waist/upper hips comfortably. If it's too small, just stretch it out!

Lay the pleated skirt on the ground. Take the bottom hem of the cut tee shirt (where it was factory-stitched) and place that on the outside of your tube of pleats all the way around, covering the raw edge of the skirt. Pin in place. Turn it inside out and, using the same color thread as your tee shirt fabric, stitch the tee shirt to the pleated skirt with a backstitch. Turn right side out and roll the top edge of the tee shirt "waistband" down a little.

Slip it on and reveal your new flirty skirt to the world.

Alternate Method: Imagine, if you will, finding a rainbow-covered pillowcase at a thrift store. You bring it home and wash it lovingly. But, alas, it clashes with your room décor! What to do, what to do? Make a skirt out of it! If you space your pleats far enough apart, you can take a funny pillowcase and make it into this pleated skirt. Start by opening up both long seams of the pillowcase (but keeping the short seam intact) with a seam ripper or scissors. Iron it flat and continue with the pleated skirt directions.

Alternate Method II: Instead of a tee shirt waistband, cut the drawstring waistband off of an old pair of sweats. Don't want to wreck a nice worn-in pair? Hit the thrift store and buy a pair of sweats just for this purpose!

Project #5:
The Tie Skirt

I have a fascination with men's ties. Soft silky ones, elegant country-club ones, funky polyester ones—you name it, I love 'em. But what's a girl to do with a bunch of ties?

Make a skirt out of 'em! But you need lots of them to do it right. This skirt is a little more labor-intensive than any other project in this book. You'll have to log in some serious sewing hours here. It's not hard, just a touch tedious. But in the end, you'll have not just a skirt, but a work of art.

What You Need

● A lot of ties (here's the math: your average tie is about 2 1/2 to 3 inches wide at the point where we're going to cut it; measure your waist loosely and divide that number by 2.5 to be safe—that's how many ties you'll need, plus one for the waistband, give or take a tie)

- Needle and lots of thread

- Pins (small safety pins or straight pins)

- One zipper, 7 to 10 inches long

- Scissors

- Tape measure

The How-To

Here is the beauty of sewing with ties: They are constructed with two layers of fabric and a lining, too. "Sew what?" you say. Well, the thing is, you can sew the ties together without ever poking that needle through the outer layer of fabric. And that means your stitches will never show! Just take your time, being careful not to poke the needle all the way through the tie, and you're good to go.

Lay out all your ties, side by side, leaving the one for the waistband aside. Position them in the order you like. The final seam will be a side seam, so plan accordingly, placing the ties you want in the front of the skirt lined up at the far right of your line of ties.

when looking for ties

at the thrift shop, you could pick a color scheme and go for it. You could go on a mission to buy only ties that are black and white, or you could look for just stripes (of any color) or polka dots (big and small). or you could just pick up ties you like that have no central theme whatsoever!

Take your tape measure and determine how long you would like your skirt to be. It depends on how tall you are, but 12 to 16 inches is usually standard for a long mini. Add 1 inch to your number, then measure the first tie from the bottom point to your determined number and cut. Cut straight across all your ties so that they are all the same length. Take the tie scraps and put them aside—we'll use them later.

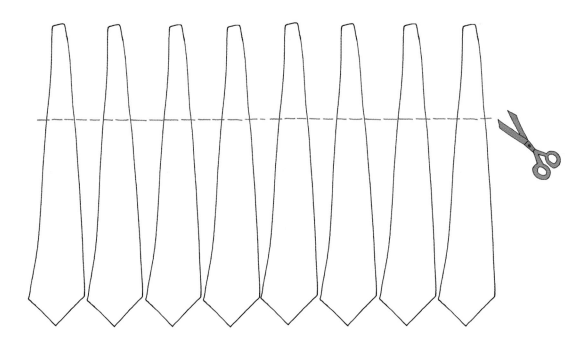

Now turn over your ties, one by one, so they stay in their designated places. Pin them together from the back, taking care not to puncture the front of the tie. Tiny safety pins work well for this, but straight pins will work too. Start stitching your ties together, again being careful not to push the needle through the front of each tie. Sewing your stitches in an angled zigzag pattern will work great, a sort of variation on the straight stitch. It will take some time to sew each and every tie together, but go slow so that you do not create any puckering or wrinkles along the way. Sew them all together flat, but hold off sewing the last two ties together just yet. When done, you can iron your seams on a **very** gentle setting to flatten them out.

Now hold up your "flat" of ties and wrap it around your waist. Does the skirt fit all the way around? If not, you'll need to add additional ties. Once you've got the skirt the perfect width, we need to add the zipper and sew up the final seam.

Nab that zipper. Look at it, caress it, work it, get to know it. Note how the zipper doesn't actually go all the way to the top of the zipper placket—there is a smidge of extra room. That's good.

Line up the top of the placket with the top of the ties and make sure the front of the zipper is on the same side as the front of the ties. Pin one side of the zipper placket to the outer edge of the tie that is last in your flat of ties. Now bring the outer edge of the other "end tie" around and pin that to the other side of the zipper placket. From the outside of the skirt, your zipper should be hidden behind the ties.

Zip and unzip your zipper a few times, making sure it works smoothly. Then, while it's still pinned, slip the skirt on with the zipper at your left side. Does it go on easily? When zipped up, does it fit your hips nicely? If the answer is yes, you're ready to finish this baby up. Sadly, if your answer is no, you must take some time to readjust the zipper, possibly adding or removing a tie. But you're almost done, so don't fret.

Turn the skirt inside out and sew the zipper in place, once again taking care not to poke the front of the ties. Finish the seam below the zipper as you had closed up the previous ties.

Now all that is left is the waistband. Take that last tie, wrap it around your waist, and center it with the excess falling to the left side, just above the zipper. The end of the tie will make a cute tie belt, see? Pin it in place. Turn the skirt inside out and stitch the top edges of all those ties to the inside of the "waistband" tie, again being careful not to poke all the way through to the front of the ties. Do not sew the waistband tie to the piece of fabric above the zipper.

Unzip the skirt. Slip it on. Zip it up. Tie the waistband into a loose knot and let the excess fall toward the floor. Spin around. Call all your friends. You just made a very fancy, one-of-a-kind tie skirt!

Doodad It

I found a tie I loved, but it had a small stain. I still bought it and incorporated it into my skirt. I simply covered the blemish with a felt flower. It looked so good, the next time I made a skirt, I added a felt flower just for the heck of it. For the down-low on felt flowers, see the section on them in Chapter 11.

● ● ● ●

What to Do with Extra Tie Parts

The skinny end part of the tie is very useful. Usually a fantastic print, it's already sewn into a lovely, neat double-layer strip of glorious fabric fashion. Add a couple of extras here and there, and you can make any number of wondrous accessories.

. . . .

Tie Choker #1: Hold the scrap piece of tie around your neck and cut it to a length that is 4 inches longer than what comfortably fits, choker-style. Cut only one end so that you keep the cool, small pointy end intact. Hem the cut side at an angle that mirrors the opposite end.

Cut a piece of Velcro into a 1-inch square. Take the fuzzy piece and sew it on (fuzzy side out) to the back side of the tie, 2 inches from the original pointy edge. Sew your felt flower where you just sewed that Velcro strip, but on the outer side of the tie. Now wrap it around your neck and make note with your finger where the underside of the tie crosses the outer side of the tie at your neck. Sew the pointy piece of the Velcro in that spot, so that when you wrap the choker around your neck, it will stick to the fuzzy Velcro.

Put it on and feel glamorous!

Tie Choker #2: Measure around your neck comfortably, then add an inch to that number. Cut your scrap of tie so that it is that length. Sew up the cut end. Cut a 1-inch square of Velcro.

Sew the pointy piece (pointy side out) to the newly hemmed end on the outer face of the tie. Sew the fuzzy side of the Velcro to the underside of the opposite end of the tie. Sew a felt flower either in the center or off to one side.

Strap it on and marvel at your chicness.

. . . .

Tie Wrist Corsage Cuff:
Follow the same exact method as that for Tie Choker #2, except this accessory will adorn your arm instead of your neck. The piece of tie will be shorter. Measure accordingly.

. . . .

Tie Headband: Most ties arsewn down on the back side so as to create a "pocket" or a "tube." If you can poke a pencil down the inside of your tie scrap and it pops out the other end, you're halfway done with this project. If you can't, you'll need to open up the tie's stitches so you can poke that pencil through and then, with just a couple of stitches here and there, close up the back side of the tie, leaving a hole all the way through. Cut a piece of elastic that is long enough to go around your head (from the top, down behind your ears, to the back of the nape of your neck). Pull the elastic a little tight, but not so tight that you cut off all circulation to your body. Cut the tie the same length as the elastic. Feed the elastic through the hole or "chute" in the tie (attach to a pencil if need be) and then knot your elastic.

Slide your new headband on and admire handy work and a new, modern preppy look.

. . . .

Tie Sunglasses Case: This is a great project for a nearly whole tie, and it also makes a great gift. Measure 8 inches from the tip of the widest edge of the tie bottom. Can you turn the tie inside out? If you can't, rip the small stitches out that are stopping you. You can sew some more back in later. Turn the tie inside out and close up the cut edge with a simple straight stitch. Turn it right side out again and attach a very small piece of fuzzy Velcro to the inner point. Fold this point down toward the back side of the tie, then sew the rough piece of Velcro to the spot where they meet. Make sure there are no seams in the way of your newly created pocket; and if you need to remove any (or fix any you ripped earlier), simply sew them back together, but remember to sew through only the back layer of fabric. Attach a felt flower to the outside.

Handy **and** dandy!

Wrap it lovingly in tissue paper, present it to a friend, and soak in their immense gratitude.

CHAPTER TEN

pants & shorts

. . . .

Project #1: Becoming Cargos

You can take any boring ol'
pair of khakis and make them
cargos by adding pockets
ripped from a pair of
unflattering jeans. If you
don't have an extra pair of
jeans lying around that you
don't wear anymore, pick
up a pair at the local
thrift. If all else fails,
you could make pockets
with spare fabric
that you have lying
around. Simply cut
the classic pocket
shape and proceed
as directed.

What You Need

- A pair of ordinary and rather plain pants
- Back pockets from an old pair of jeans (removed with a seam ripper and/or scissors)
- Needle and thread
- Pins
- Scissors

The How-To

Position one of the back pockets over the side seam right above the knee. Pin in place. Sew along the sides and bottom of the pocket. Repeat on the other leg with the remaining pocket.

Doodad It

Add ribbon trim along the tops of the new pockets. Add even more pockets. Add patches to make them extra fancy. Take denim scraps and add denim cuffs to the hem of the pants. Or sew a long piece of ribbon around the circumference of the hem of each leg and tie the excess ribbon into a bow.

Whatever you do, the end result will be completely unique and unlike any other person's pants. And that is something to be happy about. Wear your new pants proudly!

- - - -

Project #2: Pegging Pants

Pegging pants means slimming the legs. This look was huge in the eighties, and everyone—including boys—wanted their pants pegged. Fashion is cyclical, girls, and pegged pants will be back on the runways in no time! Get a jump on the trend by doing it yourself. There is no denying this would be easier if you had a sewing machine. But it's certainly not impossible without.

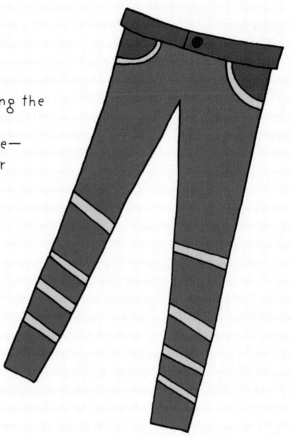

What You Need

- A pair of pants that have wider legs than you desire
- Needle and thread
- Pins
- Scissors
- A mirror to check yourself out in

The HOW-TO

Turn the pants inside out. Slip them on. Yank on each leg, pulling the excess fabric away from your leg. Where does the extra fabric begin? At the upper thigh? At the knee? Wherever it begins is where you want to start your "slimming." Take the pants off and start pinning the fabric at a slight angle so that it will hug your leg slightly. Pin all the way to the ankle in a smooth, angled line. Repeat on the other leg.

Turn the pants inside out very carefully to reveal the new shape of your pant legs. Slip them back on very gingerly (remember, they're loaded with pins!). Make sure you like the slim line of the leg and the way the pants fit. Are the legs evenly pegged? If you're not satisfied, take them off (careful—the pins!), turn them back inside out, toss them back on, and readjust your pin handiwork. If they are fitting divinely, slip them off (do I need to remind you of the pins again?) and turn them inside out again.

Starting at the top pin of one of the legs, poke your needle through both layers of the pants exactly in line with your pin. Continue with a backstitch all the way down the leg to the ankle. Knot your thread when you're all done.

Now nab those scissors and cut off the excess fabric that is on the outside of your new side seam. Cut along the line, leaving half an inch behind—no more, no less. With the pants still inside out, open up that half-inch seam allowance and spread it flat. Iron this down for a nice, clean seam. And then repeat the whole job on the other leg.

• • • •

Project #3: Making Flares

Forget pegging—you want your jeans to flare at the ankles.
No sweat!

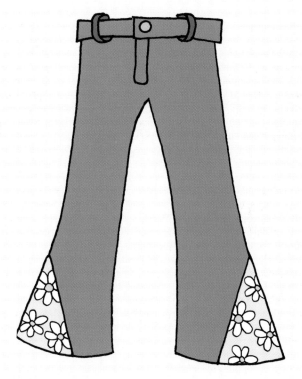

What You Need

* A pair of jeans or pants that you wish had wider legs

* A half yard of scrap fabric

* Needle and thread

* Scissors

* Pins

* Seam ripper

* Steam-A-Seam or other fusible web tape

The How-To

Using the seam ripper, open the outer side seam of your pant leg, starting at the ankle and continuing up 12 inches. Repeat on the other leg's outer side seam.

Cut two triangles out of your scrap fabric. Each should be about 13 inches tall and 6 inches in width at the widest part. Hem the bottom of each triangle by folding it up half an inch and ironing it with a strip of fusible web tape or sewing it with a hemstitch.

Turn your jeans or pants inside out, with the split seam of one pant leg facing up. Place the triangle, back side of the fabric facing up, on top of the split seam. Line up the bottom hem of the triangle with the bottom hem of the pant and the sides of the triangle with the edges of the split seam. Pin in place. Repeat on the other pant leg. Sew the triangles to the jeans or pants. Turn the pants right side out. Try them on and skip around your room in delight.

Doodad It

If you leave them as is, your pants will fray a little around your triangle of fabric. You can cover that up with just a little bit of ribbon or fancy trim. Cut it to the right length, plus an inch to fold under at the bottom of each pant leg, and stitch in place.

● ● ● ●

Project #4:
Who Wears Short Shorts?

You could cut any pair of pants off above the knee and sport a quick, albeit sloppy cutoff short. Or you can follow the directions below and, in just a touch more time, have a pair of shorts even your grandma would be proud of.

What You Need

- A pair of pants or jeans that fit you fine but have perhaps become too short or too boring

- 1 foot of ribbon

- Two large buttons

- Pins

- Scissors

- Needle and thread

- Tape measure

- Iron

The HOW-TO

Try the pants on and decide how long you would like your shorts to be. Put a pin in each pant leg, marking your desired length. Take the pants off. Measure 4 inches down from your pins, then place another set of pins there. Cut straight across the legs at those second pins. Then remove all the pins.

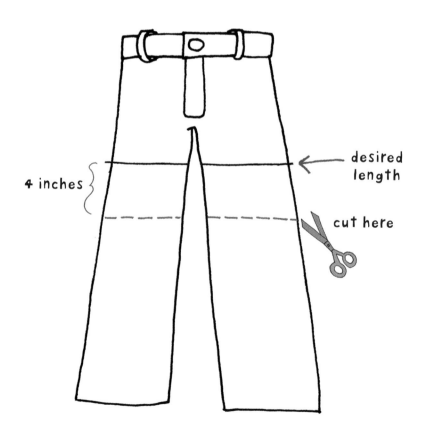

4 inches

desired length

cut here

Turn the iron on a medium setting. Fold each pant leg up 2 inches. Iron this fold in place. Fold each leg again, 2 inches, and iron it down. You now have a crisply ironed, twice-folded, 2-inch cuff.

Cut your ribbon into two 6-inch pieces. Stick one end of one piece of ribbon inside a leg at the side seam and wrap it round to the outside so it ends just above the cuff. Pin it in place, making sure to secure the ribbon on the inside and the out. Nab a button and position it on top of the ribbon, just above the cuff. Poke the needle from the inside out, through both layers of ribbon and the button. Now thread back down through the hole. Repeat this several times until it's all tight and sturdy. Knot the thread on the inside and repeat on the other leg.

● ● ● ●

CHAPTER ELEVEN

adorning your clothes with goodies

Reconstructing your clothes is good crafty fun, but so is decorating them. This chapter should inspire you to go a step further and really bedeck your clothes with flirty frills, fancy flowers, and all-around fun findings.

When I'm in a thrift store or at a garage sale (my favorite weekend activity), I always look for the sewing section. This may sound like a cliché, but there are a lot of lovely old ladies hoarding notions ("notions" is another word for generic sewing paraphernalia). I've found ancient packages of lace and trim for a quarter a bag, boxes of pins for a dime, and cans of sequins and buttons for less than a buck. Pick this stuff up when you see it supercheap and store it in your sewing kit. Then when you come across a shirt in need of some fancifying, you'll have the goods to make it happen!

Old Art, New Tee

Do you have a tee shirt you've outgrown but can't get rid of because it has a great graphic on the front? Perhaps you've found a supersassy tee at the thrift store, but you just couldn't get it over your head, no matter how hard you tried? Here's the fix: Cut the graphic out of the front of the tee and stitch it to another. Use fusible web tape to help make the old piece of tee stiffer, which will in turn make it easier to sew down. Cut a piece of fusible web tape the same size as your tee shirt graphic and stick it to the back. Then stick that whole piece down on a new tee shirt. Grab some bright embroidery thread and a needle, and stitch all the way around the edges of the graphic. When you've gone all the way around, knot the thread on the inside.

Voila, a sassy graphic tee that **fits.**

Felt Flowers, Two Ways

Method #1: Wool felt is better than those squares you can get at the craft store, but any kind will do. Cut five to seven petals, about this shape:

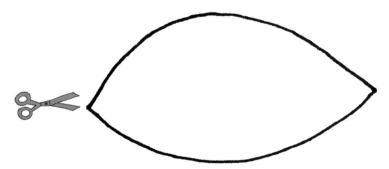

They should all be the same size. Take your needle and thread and, starting from the underside of the first petal, poke through the bottom edge and come back down on the opposite bottom edge of the petal. Now that the petal is on your thread, simply glide it down to the bottom of your thread and let it hang there until you've repeated this step with all the petals. When you're finished, tie the ends of the thread together, pulling tight. Instant flower!

For extra magic add a button to the center. You can use colorful embroidery thread to outline the petals. You can layer one flower upon another. And then you can attach them with a few stitches to just about anything.

Method #2: This works really well with velvet and with other slightly thick fabrics, too. You can even create flowers this way out of ordinary cotton fabric, but you'll need more layers, and beware, they will fray a little (which actually looks quite nice).

Cut three to four 3-inch circles of fabric, then another three to four 2-inch circles of fabric. Your results look exceptional when you alternate two different fabrics. Put your largest circles on the bottom, right side of fabric facing up, and then pile your smaller circles on top of those, making sure not to line the circles up perfectly. You want them a little askew. If you want leaves, add two leaf-shaped pieces of felt or fabric to the bottom of the stack.

Starting from the bottom underside of the stack, poke your needle, threaded with embroidery thread, up through the center of the flower. Make a small stitch in the center and come back down through the stack. Repeat, forming a small X in the center of the flower. Tie a knot. Rethread your needle and once again start from the underside of the flower and poke upward through the stack, but this time go through all the layers **except the top**. Bring the needle back down about a quarter of an inch away from the center, toward the outer edge of the flower petals, then pull tightly. Knot at the bottom of the flower, but do not cut just yet. Repeat this last step, poking the needle through all the layers but the top layer, and this time make your quarter-inch stitch in a different direction. Pull tight and knot. Do this two more times, each time stitching in a different direction. This gives the flower its curved shape and dimension.

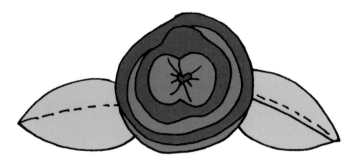

When you're all done, you can add seeds to the center with tiny beads, a button, or even a fake pearl post earring. Take the flower in your palm and kind of scrunch it up. This will give it even more curl and shape. Now use it to adorn your ballet shoes, sweaters, tees, shorts, skirts, belts, ties, chokers, wristbands, book bags—anything!

Easy Iron-on Patches

You can turn almost any fabric into an iron-on patch. Why care about iron-on patches? Because they're so easy and so useful. If you have a hole, just cover it up with a cute iron-on. A stain? Iron-on. An ugly, drab shirt or boring pair of pants? Iron-on.

We'll be using that handy-dandy fusible web tape again—more specifically, fusible web tape for appliqué, which comes in a wide roll (or by the yard). Cut a piece of fabric, then cut a piece of the double-sided fusible web tape to the same size. Remove one side of the paper from the web tape to reveal the sticky part and adhere it to your fabric. Iron it.

Now cut out the shape you want. A classic square, perhaps? Or you can get fancy and cut a more unique shape. Because there is still one side of paper backing attached, it makes the fabric stiffer and therefore easier to cut. So it's not hard to cut out letters, stars, hearts, even a little piggy, if you so desire. When you've got the shape you'd like, remove the last piece of paper, position it on your piece of clothing, and iron away.

Don't use iron-ons just for covering holes or stains. You can create designs to iron on your tee shirts too, taking them from plain to fancy in mere minutes!

With fusible web tape, you can also attach fake flowers, felt appliqués, sequins, even beads. As you've probably figured out by now, this stuff is magic and truly wonderful if you are afraid of needles.

Felt Appliqué

Felt doesn't fray. Felt has a great texture. Felt has a retro look. Felt rocks. Felt, however, isn't easy to wash. It's not that you can't wash felt creations, it's just that you have to wash them in cold water, on the delicate cycle of the machine—and you really shouldn't put them in the dryer. I'd recommend hand washing, actually.

Japanese-style cartoon animals make great subjects for felt appliqué because they are crafted of simple shapes. Cut out your design with sharp scissors. Sew the shapes together with contrasting embroidery thread and large straight stitches. Once your design is complete, you can sew it to your tee shirt (or skirt hem or jacket or sweater). A little bit of fusible web tape will keep the appliqué secure on the fabric while you sew. Stitch along the edges of the design, all the way around, and tie the thread off in a knot on the inside of the garment.

stenciling clothes

Stencils are a supremely cool way to add some color and original design to otherwise boring clothing like tee shirts, denim skirts, pant legs, cotton skirts—you name it. But, alas, the fabric paint and stencils you'll find at your neighborhood craft store probably leave something to be desired. The stencils will look like something your grandma would decorate her wall with, and the paint is goopy, globby, and comes in all the wrong colors. Our way of stenciling (mostly) avoids the cheesiest aisle in the craft store and allows for extreme creativity!

First, let's address the stencil. The aforementioned letters (see Project #7: The Scrabble Tee, in Chapter 6) you'll find at any drugstore or craft store are cool. They're cheap, too, so pick up a couple sets of same-size, same-shape letters so you can spell stuff out without having to move the **A** or the **E** when you need two of them in the same word. Cut out each letter and tape them together to make one large stencil of an entire word or even an entire phrase.

As for stenciling pictures, if you've got a computer and an art program, you can take almost any graphic photo or picture, convert it to a grayscale image, and bump up the contrast so that it's all black and white. Print it (acetate sheets are best for printing, found at an office supply store; if not, thick paper will suffice), then very carefully cut out the black parts of the high-contrast picture with an X-Acto knife.

No art program? Hit one of the many Web sites that feature stencils. There are sites devoted to cool stencils, and they feature free downloadable stencils that you just print and cut, directions included. Search for "stencils" online to get a long list of great resources.

Now on to the painting!

What You Need

- A firm 3-inch roller from the hardware or art store

- Fabric medium or textile medium (this is the only thing you "need" to get from the craft store—it's not too expensive and can usually be found near the art paint; it's white and comes in a classic plastic bottle with squirt top; and it's the stuff that makes ordinary paint stick to fabric)

- Cheap acrylic paint in your favorite colors

- An old spoon

- An old plastic plate

- Masking tape

The HOW-TO

Find a clean, nonbreezy spot outside. Set up all your supplies. Lay the tee shirt out flat on a table or the ground. Put something hard inside the shirt, like a piece of a box cut to fit in the shirt or just a flat piece of old cardboard. If you don't have anything like this, try slipping this very book inside (but read all the directions first!). You just want something that will separate the front and back layers of the shirt and that will also provide you with a firm, flat surface to work on. Position the stencil on the shirt where you'd like it and tape it down. Tape it all the way around, so as to avoid getting paint around the edges.

Mix one part textile medium to one part paint on your old plate, with your old spoon. That means if you put 2 tablespoons of paint down, put 2 tablespoons of textile medium down. Stir this mixture well. Roll the roller in the paint, coating it evenly and smoothly.

Start rolling the paint in the outside inner rim of the stencil and move toward the center. Do not push hard, do not use too much paint, and take your time. Once you've coated the holes in your stencil, lay down the roller and carefully pull up the taped stencil. The fabric medium gets real sticky right quick, so you don't want to leave the stencil on for too long.

Let it dry. This won't take very long. If you want to create a layered effect, as soon as the paint is dry, you can repeat this process with a new stencil and/or a different color. Get creative—the design can be simple or complex.

When you're completely finished and the paint is good and dry, take a clean dishtowel and place it over the painted shirt; iron the towel on a medium setting. This "sets" the paint. Always remember to wash your stenciled shirts, jeans, and skirts in cold water to prevent fading.

Other Ways to Adorn Your Tees

Look out for this fantastic **iron-on transfer** paper that you can buy for your computer printer. Print any photo (or scan a drawing you did of your best friend) on to this ingenious paper, and you can then iron it on to a blank tee! I'm hooked on this stuff.

Pin **tiny bows** made from scraps of ribbon randomly across the front of any tee. Pin small, inexpensive charms to another tee. So pretty!

Tees can be glamorous too. Sew **sequins** of various colors to your tees. Sew them in a pattern or just randomly. Sew them to the collar of a polo shirt for a diva-preppy look.

Sew a handful of **buttons** down the front of a tee shirt to resemble a classic button-down shirt placket.

Sew **lace** or **ribbon trim** to the neckline and sleeves of any tank, tee, or sweater with a tiny straight stitch. Or add trim to the inside of the neck or sleeves so it just peeks out at the edges. Do this with a hidden hemstitch.

Strings of plastic beads are sold by the yard at most fabric stores. Buy a couple of yards and drape them back and forth across the front of the tee shirt, securing them at the shoulders with a couple of tiny (but sturdy) stitches.

Embroidering tee shirts is actually a pain because the tee shirt fabric is so stretchy. But if you keep your design simple and small, a little bit of embroidery thread can go a long way and not get too mucked up. Take a permanent marker and write a word like "Love" or "Smart" in script across the front. Take some embroidery floss and, starting from the inside of the tee shirt, make tight straight stitches all along your pen mark.

Even easier than embroidering a tee shirt is **embroidering a sweater**. A knit sweater already has holes for you to poke the needle and thread through. Start from the inside of the sweater and create a large star out of six lines that cross in the center.

Scarf buckles! You can still find these quirky little things at craft stores and garage sales. These are sort of "belt buckle-esque" in nature, and their original use was to keep a ladies' neck scarf neatly in place without a knot. I always pick them up whenever I find them because they are great. How do I use them? I tuck the side hem of a bulky or ill-fitting tee shirt into the buckle, over the center bar, and back down through the buckle, and then I pull. It cinches in the shirt at my waist, sometimes exposing just a hint of skin and giving the shirt a whole new shape. And a scarf buckle comes out easily when I want to wash my shirt or use it on another poor-fitting tee.

Black permanent markers, like Sharpie pens, write fairly effortlessly on tee shirt cotton and hold up wash after wash. Try writing out a message with bubble letters or drawing a picture on the front of a tee shirt. Pull the fabric taut while you draw or write. Then, using a small brush, go back with either fabric paint or acrylic paint mixed with fabric medium (which you met when we stenciled) and paint the inside of the black lines with your paint.

Try your hand at **preschool art** again. Get a pack of what are called "transfer fabric crayons" from your local craft emporium and draw a picture on regular ol' white paper. You then iron your picture, facedown, on to a tee shirt. But follow the directions on the package so you don't set the paper, and the house, on fire!

You have a tee shirt that is your size, but it just doesn't fit so great...

· ·

You have a cool tee shirt, but it's just a teeny bit too tight...

· ·

You have a tee shirt that is mighty fine but, alas, one or two sizes too big...

· ·

You have a hip tee shirt, but it's simply giant...

· ·

You have jeans (or pants or khakis) that have become too short but otherwise fit...

CHAPTER TWELVE

the chart

So you've got an extra-large shirt that has a cool design, but you don't know where to start. Or maybe you have a great-fitting tee, but it's B-O-R-I-N-G. Check it out: Below is a handy chart. If you've got a shirt that needs some help—or a sweater or a scarf—just glance below and let the chart point you to the perfect project!

You have a tee shirt that fits nicely, but is plain and ordinary...

You have a tee shirt that is your size, but it's cut straight...

the outro

* *

Oh Lovely Reader, My Fashionista Friend,

I hope I have armed you with new knowledge that is, at this very moment, surging and pulsating through your veins and inspiring you to enter heretofore-unknown realms of fashion creativity! Creating new things out of old—making art—is stupendous fun, and it's made that much better when you can show off your work on a daily basis, just by donning new clothes.

The next book in this series challenges the same part of your brain—the "alterior crafticus modernicus"—pointing you in the direction of a whole new room. We'll cover every corner, every angle, every speck, unearthing bright new ways to spice, to spruce, and to spotlight your bedroom!

I honestly and truly had so much crazy fun creating the projects in this book, and I hope you have as good a time as I did. Keep rockin' the crafty ship, exploring your own ideas, and sharing them with your friends...and the world!

Rock on,
clea

You have a tank top that fits but is otherwise unexciting...

You have a ho-hum sweater...

You have a supercool square scarf...

You have a supersweet long scarf...

You have a muncha-buncha men's ties...